Grumblings of the Soul

Grumblings of the Soul

Depression, a Natural Response of the Body

J. GARDY BRUNO

RESOURCE *Publications* · Eugene, Oregon

GRUMBLINGS OF THE SOUL
Depression, a Natural Response of the Body

Resource Publications
An Imprint of Wipf and Stock Publishers
199 W. 8th Ave., Suite 3
Eugene, OR 97401

www.wipfandstock.com

PAPERBACK ISBN: 978-1-6667-3509-3
HARDCOVER ISBN: 978-1-6667-9182-2
EBOOK ISBN: 978-1-6667-9183-9

Contents

ACKNOWLEDGEMENTS

WHEN I WROTE THIS book in 2010, I was experiencing a very difficult moment in my life. God has since pulled me out of the pit, and I am now living a new life in Christ. He wanted me to live and taste the desert before leading me to teach others to survive and thrive in it.

Special thanks to the Lord for the inspiration and his love; all glory and honor to him alone. I also want to thank Dr. William Spencer from Gordon Theological Seminary for his encouragement and support, my brothers and sisters, Willy, Yolene, and Marie E. Frankel for their prayers and encouragement.

This book is also a tribute to my wife Ernise, and my four children, Marlie, Eunice, Sara, and Gardy who wholeheartedly supported me during the long process of writing this book while being a father. I praise the Lord for such a wonderful family.

I am truly grateful!

PREFACE

Dear Reader,

Thank you for the encouragement; upon your request, I am putting out this new edition still believing it to be one of the most challenging subjects that are affecting our culture today.

There is a difference between a depressed and a thirsty soul and the Bible has a lot to say about it. Many around the world are exposed to the word of God, but are deaf to the cry of the soul. This book will teach how to answer the cry of the soul while helping nurture your relationship with the Lord.

Open your heart and let the message of this book transform you to the glory of God.

Truly,

J. Gardy

WHY THIS BOOK?

Ten years ago, God opened my eyes to an event that had taken place around me indifferently time and time again. One morning, a young lady walked into my department and sat at a table not too far from me; she looked stressed and worried. Her headset was playing a song that was so loud that I was able to hear the tune at the distance where I was. She was like someone who was trying to conceal a bad odor with perfume, she was moving her head to the rhythm of the song, but her face betrayed her and still reflected a troubled soul. In her effort to find another solution, she suddenly got up, walked out the door, opened her purse, and pulled out a pack of cigarettes; she lit one and smoked it within minutes. Thirty minutes later, she was at the door again for another one, and another, and another. While looking at her, I remembered the word of Isaiah:

> Why spend money on what is not bread, and labor on what does not satisfy? Listen, listen to me and eat what is good and your soul will delight in the richest of fare. (Isaiah 55:2)

INSPIRATION

The political and cultural pressure that followed the French Revolution of 1789 gave birth to a socio-political reform that transformed the culture for many generations. This movement almost completely reversed the neoclassicism of the eighteenth century and became a cultural revolution where emphasis on reason and tradition was replaced by imagination, emotion, and nature. Melancholy, sentiment and passion became the benchmarks of the new era that came to be known as the Romantic Movement. Without any apparent reason, a person affected becomes very depressed, profoundly discouraged, and sad, with a great distaste for life. Chateaubriand was among the protagonists of this movement. In his autobiography "Rene," he writes:

> Atlas!... this hatred of life that I felt since my early years became stronger... I fought for some time against that evil, but indifferently without a strong resolution to win. Now, unable to find a remedy to that strange wound of my heart that was nowhere and everywhere, I decided to give up life."[1]

He didn't commit suicide but seems to have attempted it in his adolescence. Many events contributed to making melancholy the central theme in Chateaubriand's works. In the first of his 42-volume "Memoirs from Beyond the Grave", published after his death, he stated:

1. René Chateaubriand, *Les Grands Ecrivains Français* (New York: Holt, Rinehart and Watson, 1965), 482.

"My brother perished on the scaffold, my two sisters departed their painful lives after many years spent languishing in prison, and my two uncles didn't leave enough to pay for the four planks of their coffins. As for myself, literature has caused me both joy and sorrow, and I don't despair, God willing, of dying in the poorhouse."[2]

The hopelessness and despair in these specific passages are almost palpable. The author sees life as a burden, a painful pilgrimage that is not to be challenged but to be accepted and embraced as a fate; a "bonheur d'être triste" *(happiness to be sad)*. The mastery and lyricism that are used in describing the most tragic moment give him the title of father of French Romanticism. In his autobiography, he painted a picture of an adolescent who hated life and that hatred became stronger over the years. He seemingly began to fight against that enemy but indifferently; he later said that he was fighting: *"Without a strong resolution to win."* His own prognostic four decades later was to finish almost like his siblings, in a poorhouse. He was not the only one in his generation to have been infected with this virus; one of his late contemporaries Alfred de Musset in his sonnet "Sadness" wrote:

"I have lost my strength and my life, my friends and my joy… the only thing that remains for me in life is to have shed tears."[3]

The author lost everything that was precious to him: life, friends, joy, etc., but, yet, he has something that he still holds dear to his heart and won't let go of: it is the power to shed tears, his sanctuary, a haven where he can find solace and comfort. Sadness was becoming so pandemic that it was nicknamed: "Le mal du siècle." Loneliness became a necessity. Everyone was in a "self-inflicted quarantine where tears were the only confidant. That state of mind was affecting every community without any apparent stressor to explain it. The depression of these people was not

2. René Chateaubriand, *Memoirs Beyond the Grave* (New York: NYREV, Inc. 2018), 17.

3. Alfred de Musset, *Tristesse*, Gauthier, 530.

caused by psychotic or psychoneurotic disorder as it came to be known; in fact, there was no disconnection from reality, delusions, or incomprehensible talk in the life of the affected individual. Ironically, the initiators were philosophers, intellectuals, ambassadors, members of the French academy and others. It was a self-inflicted, make-believe type of stressor where the focus was on the writer's emotions and his inner world.

That Age of Reason, or Enlightenment Philosophy, rejected the authority of both the monarchy and the Catholic Church for the promotion of a new society based on emotion. There was no psychological or psychosocial form of stress that could justify "Le mal du siècle". The cause was an alienation from the world, a malady that mostly affected the male segment of the population. By the mid-nineteenth century, it had become a way of life, an 'état d'âme.' That gloomy spirit was now present not only in the mood of the culture but idealized in the literature.

In this twenty-first century we are witnessing a rebirth of this misery of the heart and many doctors and psychologists report a continual increase in the number of people experiencing symptoms of depression; they agree that it is more than just the result of a "chemical imbalance in the brain". In fact, in a book titled: *Inflammation and Immunity in Depression*, Pahlajani and Najjar state that:

> "Clinical and experimental evidence suggests a multifactorial etiology, emphasizing the need for important paradigm shifts in the neurobiology of depression extending beyond a "chemical imbalance."[4]

Steve Rathje, in *Psychology Today*, goes further; he states that if we continue to see mental illness as a brain disease (chemical imbalance) and solely refer to its biological causes, then people would be more reluctant to see it as a weakness of character or psychosocial problem.[5]

---

4. S. Pahlajani S. and S. Najjar, "*Inflammation and Immunity in Depression*," Elsevier (2018).

5. See S. Rathje, "Don't Say That Depression."

SO MANY QUESTIONS

Weeping may remain for a night, but rejoicing comes in the morning.

—PSALM 30:5

Depression is addressed and defined in several different nosological categories. One type may be caused by events in someone's life, another by chemical changes in the brain. In the *Scientific Journal of Polonia University*, Szczygiet states that depression can manifest itself in different psychosomatic symptoms like feeling fatigue, weariness, or discouragement of life.[1] Furthermore, observation of people with depression seems to suggest yet one more possibility: "A desire to achieve a *"want"* that is believed to be the key to fulfillment;" something that defines someone's personality, his/her *"raison de vivre."*

First, let us turn our attention to the former. In *the Journal of the American Society of Nephrology*, PL Kimmel writes:

> "Patients may be the result of using somatic symptoms in qualifying the extent of depression."[2]

1. B. Szczygiet, B. Wanot, and M. Magerčiakova, M., "Depression Definition, History of Views, Recognition," *Scientific Journal of Polonia University*, 30(5) (2018): 99–106.

2. Kimmel, P.L., K. Weihs, and R.A. Peterson, "Survival in Hemodialysis Patients: The Role of Depression," *Journal of the American Society of Nephrology* 4 (1) (1993): 12–27.

Further, Susan Block in her book *Managing Depression*, says that:

> "No "bright line" separates depression from grief or adjustment reactions, the physician must assess whether the patient's symptoms have reached the threshold for treatment."[3]

If somatic symptoms are used in qualifying the extent of depression and there is no bright line or protocol to separate depression from grief, then when does grief ends and depression start? What standard do physicians use to medicate? What instrument do they use to assess? How do they figure out the threshold? The more we investigate the concept of depression, the more questions we generate. Since our investigation is generating more questions than answers, should we look at a different path for a solution?

It is customary for people to set goals in life that when achieved, are equated with being successful. Conversely, when the years are accumulating and the dreams are still remote or even unreachable, a sense of failure will slowly begin to overshadow that dream. Hopelessness will come to occupy the mind and eventually trigger disturbances in sleep and eating patterns. The affected individual will start to withdraw from activities that used to be pleasurable and believe that his life will never get better. He may want to be alone, avoid social gathering and even refuse to take initiative, believing that his situation is irreversible. Often, such a person will tend to seek refuge in alcohol, drugs, sexual activities, even eating disorders. In their *Group Therapy Manual*, Ricardo Nuñez and Jeanne Miranda provide a list of behaviors that are to be expected in a person with clinical depression:

A. Feeling depressed or down nearly every day.

B. Not being interested in or unable to enjoy things you used to enjoy.

C. Appetite and/or weight change.
(eating either more or less than is usual for you)

---

3. Susan Block, "Assessing and Managing Depression in the Terminally Ill Patients," *Ann Intern Med* 132 (3) (2000): 209–18.

D. Big changes in how much you sleep.
   (sleeping either more or less than is usual for you)

E. Changes in how fast you move.
   (either being fidgety and restless or slowed down)[4]

When such behaviors are evident, a depression diagnosis is imminent. Indeed, for many, it all starts with a desire. Once that desire reaches a critical level, it is now a fly caught in a spider web; the more it struggles to be free, the more entangled it gets. Something must be done or else it will get worse. By all means it must be dealt with medically and this is exactly what the medical community wants to do. In fact, Michael VonKorff, in his article *Health Care Costs of Primary Care Patients with Recognized Depression*, writes:

> "Patients diagnosed as depressed had higher annual health care costs ($4246 vs $2371, P<.001) and higher costs for every category of care..
>
> Pharmacy records indicated greater chronic medical illness in the diagnosed depression group, but large cost differences remained after adjustment ($3971 vs $2644). Twofold cost differences persisted for at least 12 months after initiation of treatment."[5]

Please underline "Twofold cost". Evidently, millions of dollars are being spent to treat this disease; unfortunately, successful treatment is very limited.

> Experts estimate that 80 to 90 percent of people who suffer depression can be significantly helped. Because of the underlying neurochemical vulnerability, however, depression tends to be a recurrent illness. Eight years after a first episode, three-fourths of the previously depressed patients will have a recurrence.[6]

4. R. F. Muñoz and J. Miranda, *Group Therapy Manual for Cognitive-Behavioral Treatment of Depression* (Santa Monica: Rand, 2000).

5. Gregory E. Simon, Michael VonKorff, and William Barlow, *Archives of General Psychiatry* 52 (10) (1995): 850–856.

6. Frank et al, *Archives of General Psychiatry* 47 (1990): 1093ff.

As recurrence of depression happens at such a high percentage, it is therefore absolutely necessary to look unto other possibilities for treatment. Professionals in the field have revealed flaws in the diagnosis process, difficulties in locating the line between grief and depression. Why are they so reluctant to try other options if the instrument of diagnosis is so unreliable? They seem to show no interest in identifying the causes of depression; rather the concern is to concentrate all effort and resources in treatment. The reason is obvious; there is more money to be had.

In Psalm 30, David suggests that sometimes emotions can behave in a cycle. A long day may end with sorrow but since God's compassion is renewed every morning (Lam. 3:23), rest assured that he will change the sorrow into joy.

> *"Weeping may remain for a night, but rejoicing comes in the morning"* (Psalm 30:5)

[A]DISCUSSION QUESTIONS

1. Has someone ever labeled you because of your emotions?

   _____

   _____

2. Have you accepted or rejected it?

   _____

   _____

3. Are you often sad? How would explain that sadness?

   _____

   _____

4. Do you have any close relatives that share your attitude?

_____

_____

5. Do you see your attitude as something inherited? If the answer is yes, how is that expressed?

_____

_____

6. Do you ever have suicidal thoughts? Have you talked to someone about it?

Describe a time when you were.

_____

_____

WHAT IS DEPRESSION?

Do not be anxious about anything
but in everything,
by prayer and petition, with thanksgiving,
present your request to God

—PHIL 4:6

An investigation of the history of depression seems to suggest a new detour since the nineteenth century. The conception of a disposition of the mind to initiate inspiration (Le mal du siècle) has changed. Melancholy, sadness, and loneliness that used to be tools to stimulate the mind have now been labeled a full-blown disease that requires treatment and therapy. Lewin in his article Réflexions sur la Dépression states that:

> "In past centuries, psychiatry has not freely used, as it does now, the term "depression" to designate a pathological set of symptoms. The literature of yesteryear spoke more of melancholy.."[1]

Many philosophers of that time have coined an idea that combines dualism, insignificance, and mastery to describe emotions like sadness and loneliness and they were desired and highly fashionable. Early in the twenty-first century, however, it has

1. Bertram D. Lewin, "Réflexions sur la dépression," *Revue Française de psychanalyse* Vol. 68 (2004/4): 1073–1084.

acquired a different connotation; "The inability to respond to a want that is considered to be very important." Better yet, "Starvation of the Soul".

Dreams seem to be a popular apparatus that everyone entertains and experiences, and they reside in a continuum between success and failure. They are the motivation that wakes you up in the morning, the mechanism that literally gets you to work and starts a new day. As long as the possibility of fulfilling that dream remains vital, life goes on. The machine will continue its trajectory into the unknown until some insensitive soul crushes the last chance to make that dream a reality. Unfortunately, that disappearance doesn't leave an empty room; to the contrary, it is quickly replaced with desolation, depression and discouragement which is a new phase in that person's life.

For a regular person, the motivation could be the love of a wife, the affection of the children, the company of a good friend, the pleasure to be at home. It could be as simple as a hobby, helping a neighbor or a destitute, putting a smile on someone's face. When the power to make that something a reality is stolen or broken beyond repair, when all efforts to reconstruct or renovate cease to be, a new emotion will begin to germinate; it is depression. Sedation with drugs or alcohol is sometimes used to silence these negative emotions but as perfumes are unable to eliminate perspiration, no substance has ever been able to camouflage depression.

Even though studies[2] have shown that these solutions are only temporary, the brief sense of pleasure they generate continues to bring people back. Besides, the consequences of such behavior can only lead to addiction.

Another group thinks that money can buy everything including satisfaction and joy; so, they live in a vicious cycle, amassing lots of money searching for joy. Since they cannot find it, they assume that it must be more expensive and try to

Why spend money on what is not bread, and your labor on what does not satisfy?
—Isaiah 55:2

2. Frank et al, *Archives*.

amass yet more money. The reality is that the more they collect, the greater the void, the disappointment and eventually the depression. Joy is like a treasure buried in a big island; it is impossible to find it without a map.

We all have embedded in our genes a craving to achieve, a desire to reach the next level; everyone goes to sleep at night contemplating the next strategies to implement so their dreams can become a reality. When there is no more goal, or obstacles to overcome, a sense of boredom will begin to invade the consciousness and the person will slowly begin to slide into depression. How many times have we heard rich people say: "Now that I reached the top, what is left for me to prove?" Or a billionaire, after being asked what else he wants since he has so much money, responds: "Just a little more." He is still chasing a shadow named: pride. Solomon was at the epic of his life when he made this remark:

> "Whoever loves money never has enough; whoever loves wealth is never satisfied with his income." (Ecclesiastes 5:10)

> I tried cheering myself with wine, and embracing folly—my mind still guiding me with wisdom. I wanted to see what was worthwhile for men to do under heaven during the few days of their lives. I undertook great projects: I built houses for myself and planted vineyards. I made gardens and parks and planted all kinds of fruit trees in them. I made reservoirs to water groves of flourishing trees. I bought male and female slaves and other slaves who were born in my house. I also owned more herds and flocks than anyone in Jerusalem before me. I amassed silver and gold for myself and the treasure of kings and provinces. I acquired men and women singers and a harem as well—the delights of the heart of man. I became greater than anyone in Jerusalem before me. In all this my wisdom stayed with me.

> I denied myself of nothing my eyes desired; I refused my heart no pleasure. My heart took delight in all work, and this was the reward for all my labor. Yet when I surveyed all that my hands had done and what I

had toiled to achieve, everything was meaningless, chasing after the wind; nothing was gained under the sun. (Ecclesiastes 2:3–11)

Solomon has gotten everything his heart desired. He has climbed the highest mountain, down the lowest pit and explored the lowest valley. He has seen and done it all; nothing seems to impress this man. He has reached the end of the maze, no more challenges to conquer, and it is beginning to be boring. Nothing motivates him to wake up in the morning or excites him. He said that nothing was worthwhile doing. He surveyed all that his hands had done and concluded that they were all meaningless, chasing after the wind. What a horrible position to be in! To find pleasure in nothing is a perfect diagnosis for depression. It is sad for someone to see life as an old redundant activity that is not worth his time. He looked at all his hard labor and called it a waste, his accomplishment, the fruit of his labor and considered them all worthless. It is important to remember that this man was the richest man on earth.

Isn't it ironic? People at the bottom of the scale are working their butt off to get to the top; they believe it to be the key to fulfillment while those on the top are depressed and disillusioned because wealth does not seem to deliver the peace of mind they are so desperately seeking. There must be something else to life than to be born, go to school, get a good job, buy whatever the heart desires, retire and die. Isn't it reasonable for people to be depressed after completing this routine? There is a more precious reason than to follow this routine.

EMOTION AND DEPRESSION

Of all God's creation, humans are the most emotional. They can naturally and instinctively reflect on their faces an event that has affected them on a personal level, without ever saying a word; it is a window that opens the inner being to the outside world. It is so revealing that people often must fake a smile or keep a straight face just to prevent a complete betrayal of their most intimate feelings. These emotions can involve things like love, hatred, guilt, sorrow, etc. Most of these emotions are secondary to something else and are considered passive; they come and go. Others however tend to hang on like a thick cloud in our blue sky; they persist and sometimes become a label of identity. Many use them to judge friends, or co-workers: "He is the proud guy, the jealous man, or the mean girl." Those that reflect a negative image are more persistent, things like: sorrow, hatred, fear, anger etc. Sorrow which normally represents a natural response to a loss can become an emotional disorder if not dealt with. The same thing is true for sadness; it is accepted as a natural emotion but when it is prolonged, it often leads to loss of appetite, inability to sleep, and even difficulty finding pleasure in what used to be fun. This, particularly, is the blurring line between the two extremes.

Everyone is advised to live a balanced life, remain in the middle lane even if it is for no other reason than to keep one's sanity. Bereaving is part of life; people may mourn the death of a friend or family member for several days and even months. It is normal, and sometimes expected and should not be mistaken for depression. Losing the love and affection of someone dear to one's heart can be devastating. As emotional creature, we will shed tears, we will have sleepless nights, we will lose our appetite, etc. Faith in God is no substitute for emotion; in fact, each one operates on its own wavelength. Many faithful servants of God were brokenhearted: David, Job, Jeremiah even Jesus. In the garden of Gethsemane, before his crucifixion, Jesus was physically, emotionally, and morally drained; he was about to face alone the most challenging time of his life. Even the prayer support of his closest friends he couldn't get; he was abandoned. Matthew wrote:

> [Jesus] began to be sorrowful and troubled. Then He said to them: "My soul is overwhelmed with sorrow to the point of death." (Matthew 26:37–38)

> "And being in anguish, he prayed more earnestly, and his sweat was like drops of blood falling to the ground." (Luke 22:44)

The word *anguish* literally means psychic and physical discomfort, born from a feeling of imminent danger. Other translations use *agony* which is extreme physical or mental suffering. The fact that Jesus was asking the father for an alternative to his sacrificial death was a clear demonstration of his humanity; he was facing the highest level of anxiety.

Emotion is a faculty that completes our humanity; it should not be subject to judgement or belittling. At the same time, one should consider seeking professional help if those emotions are affecting other aspect of his/her life; or if they are leading to contemplation of suicidal thoughts.

Sometimes it begins as a simple desire but is capable of becoming a disease when disregarded. It is not popular in the developing world but nevertheless very much present, affecting the lives of many. Unlike the nineteenth century when it was a "manmade aristocratic trick," in this era however, it is a real problem that is affecting many families. Maybe we do not hear much about it in the poor communities, it is not because of lack of evidence, but because of lack of representation. People primarily see doctors for emergencies; they are more concerned about finding their next meal than about going to hospitals for depressive symptoms. This silent killer is especially very active among adolescents and women in the poor communities and no one seems to care; it is not just a flight of the imagination. Martin E. P. Seligman says:

> "Women are twice likely to suffer depression as men are, because, on average, they think about the problems in ways that amplify depression... women tend to contemplate their depression, mulling it over and over, trying to analyze it and determine its source."[1]

That is not it. Furthermore, experts estimate that as many as fifteen percent of those that are depressed eventually resort to self-destruction.[2]

The situation is even more alarming among adolescents. Elliot S. Gershon, chief of the clinical psychogenetics branch of the National Institute of Mental Health states:

> The chilling fact is that we may be on the verge of an epidemic-like increase of mania, depression, and suicide. The trend is rising almost exponentially and shows no signs of letting up. I would go as far as to say this is going to be the public health problem of the 1990s and beyond if the trend continues.[3]

It is also important to mention that according to one study, depression among the elderly is often associated with disability, isolation, bereavement, and poverty.[4]

If this is not convincing, consider this other study that involved more than 11,000 people, published in *The Journal of the*

1. Martin E. P. Seligman, *Learned Optimism* (New York: Alfred A. Knopf, 1991), 75.

2. Anne H. Rosenfield, "Depression: Dispelling Despair," *Psychology Today* (June: 1985): 28.

3. Joseph Alper, "Depression at an Early Age," *Science* (May, 1986): 45–50. Kennedy et al. "Hierarchy of Characteristics Associeted With Depressive Symptoms in an Urban Elderly Sample," *American Journal of Psychiatry* 146(2): 220–225.

4. K.B. Wells et al., "The Functioning and Well-being of Depressed Patients," *Journal of the American Medical Association* 262(7): 914–919.

American Medical Association. It asserts that people with depression had worse physical, social, and role functioning, they were in worse physical health and suffered more bodily pain than people with chronic medical diseases such as diabetes, arthritis, back problems etc.[5]

Evidence that is so overwhelming requires proper investigation. The intent of this book is not to advise health professionals to reevaluate their practices but to awaken the Christian community to consider looking at other possible solutions to this problem.

DISCUSSION QUESTIONS

1. What motivates you to wake up in the morning?

_____

_____

_____

2. How would you feel if an obstacle stood in the way and prevented you from accomplishing your most precious dream?

_____

_____

_____

3. Do you have such an obstacle; did you find a way to avoid it, how?

_____

_____

_____

5. Frank et al., *Archives.*

4. If you couldn't avoid it, did the experience leave you with a sense of failure?

_____

_____

_____

5. How does the memory make you feel going forward?

_____

_____

_____

RELATIONSHIP AND DEPRESSION

The survival of every living creature depends on relationships. Human beings as a species, along with animals, need the nurture of parents for their wellbeing, sustainability, and growth. Life as we know it does not exist in a vacuum. Seeds will not germinate and grow to maturity without a close relationship with nature. Without nurture, our species will not continue to thrive. We are to one another the reason for joy or sadness. Someone's residence, a school, a place of worship, anyone of these domains can negatively affect someone's life to the point of complete emotional disturbance or even becoming suicidal. Conversely, a home can be the greatest source of joy and encouragement for a person. It is often said: "happiness comes from within"; after a long day at work, everyone looks forward to going into a welcome home. Loneliness can be very depressing. It feels good to be asked: "How was your day at work or at school."

It is indeed sad to enter a home after a long day of work and find no one to give you a kiss or a hug. The media wants you to believe that flipping channels, talking to *Alexa*, or some other electronic gadgets can replace the warmth of a spouse, the noise of the children or the joke of a good friend; it is a lie, there is no substitute for a good relationship. If it is depressing to live in an empty home, it is disheartening to even consider sharing a home with a quarrelsome or nagging partner. This is according to Prov. 27:15. The latter is a death sentence where the victim is slowly being brought to insanity and despair.

God said: "It is not good for man to be alone" and anyone who attempts to prove God wrong is subject to failure. Relation-

We are to one another the reason for joy or sadness

ship is a very strategic instrument in the construction of someone's life; its rejection is costly. The teacher of a classroom, for example, must have a good relationship with the children if he wants his teaching to be effective. On the other hand, he can potentially cause a child to despise school if his approach to teaching induces fear or emotional stress. Consider a child who left a loving home to attend school; for seven hours he will be sitting in front of a teacher who may be wicked and abusive. Suppose that the child cries when he/she is being taken to school in the morning, the guardian may assume that he/she "doesn't like school" and may force him/her to get out of the car. The reality is that he/she is nervous to sit in a room for seven hours with someone he/she does not feel comfortable with; this is downright torture. Likewise, a spouse can make home an oasis or the most agonizing and depressing place ever. For some people, going home after work is a reason for anxiety. They would rather stay out, embark in some extra-hour project, ask for overtime or think of any possible reason to keep them out of the house: they don't want to face the beast. The common denominator that triggers despair in all these examples is the duration.

Long term effects of an emotionally abusive relationship can be devastating to the very core of the victim. The mind can cope with stressful situations for a short period of time, but when it persists, it creates an emotional dent that can be irreversible. Prolonged stress can contribute to long term problems for heart and blood vessels which leads to an increase in heart rate, stress hormones and blood pressure. So, peace and joy take roots in a good relationship.

"It is *not good* for man to be alone…" (Genesis 2:18)

DISCUSSION QUESTIONS

1. Do you feel more comfortable around coworkers or people at home?

   _____

   _____

2. Are you anxious to go home after work or do you always look for reasons to stay longer at work?

   _____

   _____

3. Do you have anyone at home you can talk to or do you rely on the TV for company?

   _____

   _____

4. Do you eat dinner alone or with children and/or partners?

   _____

   _____

5. How much time do you spend watching TV or on the phone at home?

   _____

   _____

THE BIBLE PERSPECTIVE

"The Lord God formed the man from the dust of the ground and breathed into his nostrils the breath of life, and the man became a living being."

—GENESIS 2:7

The Bible, being a "Light in our path", has answers to many questions that trouble the world today if we only had the wisdom to consult it. In this information era, everything that is purchased is expected to come with instructions. The Food and Drug Administration requires that food be labeled. The consumer must be informed as to how to use the material or the food he has bought. Sometimes we buy stuff that are very simple to use and do not require much instruction; yet we expect to find the piece of paper inside.

The Bible is no different; it explains how God put together a world with a multitude of complex creatures that science after centuries of research is still not capable of fully comprehending the least of any category. As if that was not enough, He further created man in his image and that was the most amazing creation ever. For generations, science has been trying to get an understanding of the functioning of the smallest organ of the human body; they only were able to scratch the surface. God sees our limitations and in his mercy, He provided the Bible to help shed some light.

In the first book and first chapter, He explains the origin of man. He says:

> "Let us make man in our image, in our likeness, and let them rule over the fish of the sea and the birds of the air, over the livestock, over all the earth, and over all the creatures that move along the ground." So God created man in His image, in the image of God he created him; male and female he created them." (Genesis 1:26–27)

God is a spirit, He made man like him and the likeness in question is the spiritual image of God; so, we are a spirit, we live in a body and we have a soul. This body of ours is made of flesh, soul, and spirit. It is a trinity that cannot be divided except through death. Once death takes place, the spirit is separated from the body and no technology or science can reverse the process to put them back together again. Someone can use a pacemaker to reenergize the heart, oxygen to help the lungs; nothing can get a dead person back to life. Man is not just a machine that can be manipulated by replacing a battery or changing a fuse to get it going. We are a very complex trichotomy that can never be separated if life is to be sustained.

Only one person has the power to reunite body and soul: Jesus of Nazareth; this is confirmed in the resurrection of Lazarus. This man was four days in the tomb, there was no hope for the family to ever see him again in this world. His sisters were disillusioned, they said: "Had you been here, my brother would not have died." It was no use to importune the master because the body has already begun to decompose after four days in the tomb. Jesus answered and said:

> "Didn't I tell you that if you believe you will see the glory of God?" (John 11:40)

Jesus had the stone rolled away and after praying to his father, he called in a loud voice:

> "Lazarus, come out! The dead man came out, his hands and feet wrapped with strips of linen, and a cloth around his face (John 11:43)

People couldn't believe their eyes. Lazarus came out of the tomb. They were stunned with disbelief and rightly so; it was the first time they have witnessed something like that. If it were today, people would have reacted the same way. Everybody knows that once the soul and the body are separated, there is no magic that can reunite them. With God, everything is possible. The book of Acts says in chapter 26:8 *"Why should any of you consider it incredible that God raises the dead?"*

Lazarus was able to get out because Jesus, the Son of God, the Resurrection and the Life had called him.

The body of a dead person in a room cannot move because the spirit that makes him able to act has departed him. After God formed Adam with dirt, it remained lifeless until God blew life into it. After death, the body is back in the state it was before God blew the breath of life into its nostrils.

We are a spirit, we live in a body and we have a soul.

God, the Creator of that trinity explains in details the proper way to maintain and care for each unit. He carefully explains that they have different sources and therefore different needs. They are nurtured, fed, developed, and maintained differently. The Bible tells us that God formed man from the dust of the earth; but to invigorate that mass, He blew into his nostrils something from heaven: God's own breath.

> "The Lord God formed the man from the ground and breathed into his nostrils the breath of life, and the man became a living being." (Genesis 2:7)

Man is not just terrestrial; he is also celestial and as such, he requires two kinds of care. Paul understood that well when he said in Galatians 5:17:

> "The flesh has desires contrary to the spirit."

Jesus went further when he said in John 3:6: "Flesh gives birth to flesh, but the Spirit gives birth to spirit."

Today's conversation is about the importance of an educated mind, the proper diet to support a healthy body, the kind of exercise to look young, the educational training that would make you stand tall. People are overly concerned about providing the body with the proper nutrients, acquiring the physical energy to remain competitive, and the intellectual capacity to excel. At the least sign of discomfort, visits to specialists are secured to support and promote an optimal functioning body. All effort seems to be concentrated around that single unit. There is nothing wrong with that, Paul encourages the believer to do just that. In the book of Ephesians, we read:

> No one ever hated their own body, but they feed and care for their body, just as Christ does the church. (Ephesians 5:29)

The Bible demands that we care for the house we live in, for it is good stewardship. Since a good steward is someone who conducts, supervises, and manages responsibly something entrusted to his/her care, underfeeding as well as overfeeding disqualifies the manager as a good steward. So proper precautions should be taken to prevent that from happening. A level of holistic wellness would require an equitable balance of the physical, mental, and spiritual unit.

Any automobile consists of three sections (motor, transmission, and frame). The good functioning of this automobile requires a particular level of attention to each unit. If the transmission and the motor are well-maintained while the frame, which consists of steering and suspension knuckles, engine cradles and mounts, axle housings and covers, brakes and steering etc., is completely forgotten, this automobile would be a death trap and eventually fall apart. No one in his right mind would want to get a free ride in such a car. It is considered dangerous because one of the three units has been neglected. Likewise, the Spirit is an integral unit of the body, it needs to be fed and nurtured; depriving it of the necessary nutrients is dangerous and would lead to depression.

A holistic wellness requires an equitable balance of the physical, mental and spiritual unit.

God made man out of dirt; it is normal for the body to be attracted to things of this earth: immorality, position, extravagance, sorcery, wealth, rivalry, jealousy, pride, selfishness, sex, envy, drunkenness, prostitution, and the like. He also puts his spirit in man; that spirit also has needs. Everyone is aware of the law of attraction: "like attracts like." The fact that we are living in the material does not justify that deliberate decision to starve the spirit to death. Audible calls are constantly being made to the mind and they remain unanswered. Man came from God, he must stay connected to Him to live. The body has no appetite for things of heaven; neither will it make any requests for such. Paul in his epistle to the Romans testified of that; he said:

> When I want to do good, evil is right there with me. For in my inner being I delight in God's law; but I see another law at work in the members of my body, waging war against the law of my mind and making me a prisoner of the law of sin at work within my members. What a wretched man I am! Who will rescue from this body of death? (Romans 7:21–24)

This struggle involves two opponents as you see: the body and the spirit. These two foes have been fighting since creation and very rarely do they come to consensus. Every Christian, upon embracing the case of Christ, enters this competition. The mind which arbitrates this contest almost never sides with the spirit. The body is very demanding, and it is always pressuring the mind for more. The already soft voice of the spirit is constantly being suppressed by the carnal. People are becoming more and more accustomed to living with a starving spirit. The weight of materialism is so heavy that the whole creation has been groaning as in the pains of childbirth (Rom. 8:22). There is little to no concern for the desires of the soul. The prince of this world tips the arbiter's scale in his favor; he feeds the mind with his passion and he has no regard for a starving soul. Even the Son of God was subjected to his temptations. The Gospel of Matthew tells us that:

> Jesus after his baptism was led by the Spirit into the desert to be tempted by the devil. After fasting forty days and forty nights, he was hungry. The tempter came to

him and said: "If you are the Son of God, tell these stones
to become bread."

Jesus answered, it is written: "Man doesn't live by
bread alone, but by every word thot comes from the
mouth of God," Then the devil took him to the holy city
and had him stand on the highest point of the temple. "If
you are the Son of God," he said, "Throw yourself down.
For it is written: "He will command His angels concerning you, and they will lift you up in their hands, so you
will not strike your foot against a stone."

Jesus answered him, "It is also written: "Do not put
the Lord your God to the test." Again the devil took him
to a very high mountain and showed him all the kingdoms of the world and their splendor. "All this I will give
to you, if you will bow down and worship me."

Jesus said to him, "Away from me, Satan! For it is
written: Worship the Lord your God and serve him only."
Then the devil left him and angels came and attended
him. (Matthew 4:1–11)

The point of interest in the whole conversation here is the fact
that Jesus said to the tempter: "*Man doesn't live by bread* alone."
Please notice the word *alone;* it indicates the fact that there are
other ways of caring for the body than just feeding it with bread.
Obviously, Jesus was hungry, and the tempter was aware of that
since he asked him to turn stones into bread to satisfy his needs.
Extreme hunger can cause someone to be irritable, violent, even
inhuman. 2 Kings 6 tells us of a famine that was so severe in Israel
that the citizens began to eat donkey; when that wasn't enough,
they started to eat their own kids. The feeling of hunger and thirst
are controlled in the brain and cannot be ignored; so, the body
has its own way of telling us when it needs food or water. Without
that feeling, the body risks falling into starvation and death. This
sensation is also true for heat, cold, pain etc. Physically speaking,
the maker of this body made sure He placed into it a sophisticated
security system to detect and deal with anything that can be a challenge to its good functioning.

Now if the Creator was so careful with a body that is destined
to live for a short period of time and rot after death, why should

anyone consider it incredible that he would put yet a more complex system so the host can sense the needs of the soul that is to live eternally?

EVANGELICALS

In John 17:16, Jesus said to his disciples that they are in this world but not of this world. The world in question here is the Greek word *"Kosmos"* which means: *System, Organization.* This system is organized by the enemy to keep Christians occupied so they have no time for God. In 1 John 2:15, God gave a clear warning about the love of the world; he says:

> "Do not love the world or anything in the world."

The world was created by God for the wellbeing of his people, but Satan uses it as an instrument to turn the mind of God's children away from him; he turned everything into a system. What is a system? Well, the dictionary defines it as "A group of interacting or interrelated entities that form a unified whole." The unified whole is the world, and the different entities are the many units it is made of. We have a system of government, school system, system of music, etc. Everything is part of a system or organization and for someone to be allowed integration, he needs to conform to the standards of that unit.

The fight between the evangelicals and the secular has come to an halt. Christians have slowly put down their weapons and now work in unison with the former enemy; they are becoming part of the system. The priority for them now is to secure a position in any organization; then, try to make their faith fit its standards. Every day, they further bend the rules to satisfy new obligations. For six days they work, on the seventh, if allowed, they go to church begging God to increase their territory, or bless their business while the non-Christian goes to the beach in search of pleasure. Conformity with the system has entered a new phase; it is now in the church. If the trend continues, soon the plainfield will be leveled. The lifestyle that could have been in yesteryear repugnant in organizations has now made it into the church and the pulpit. In this post-modern world, serving God is more like a lucky charm.

> The Lord looks down from heaven on the sons of men to see if there are any who understand, any who seek God. All have turned away, all have become corrupt; there is no one who does good, not even one." (Psalm 14:2–3)

DESPAIR AND HOPE OF ETERNITY

When the cup of anxiety is overflowing, when apparently the heart seems to have reached the end of the road, hopelessness and despair becomes the new occupant of the mind.

> "Why my soul, are you downcast? Why so disturbed within me?" (Psalm 42:5)

This is in descriptive terms the expression of extreme dejection, a concerning sensation. There is a sense of compassion in this question. Lacking a better term to express his thirst, the author starts the psalm with a figurative analogy: *As the deer pants for streams of water, so my soul pants for you, my God.* Is being deprived of the presence of God truly comparable to a deer longing for water? That question can only be answered by the people to whom God has said: "...And you will know what it is to be deprived of my presence." (Numbers 14:34)

Verse 36 tells us that:

> "These men who were responsible for spreading the bad report about the land were struck down and died of a plague before the Lord."

It is a death sentence!

The psalmist was so depressed that he demanded an explanation for such sadness. *"Why is my soul so downcast?"* If eternal life is a present possession as presented in the Gospel of John, how can depression be so overwhelming in the life of a servant of God? Despair is seen as a common occurrence in the Bible; through its pages, one can find many vivid examples of dedicated men and women of God who had to struggle with depression. Someone can argue that it is acceptable because it was before the coming of the Savior. The book of Exodus for example tells how Moses, who had an assignment to lead God's people from Egypt to the promised land, was pressured to provide them with food, meat, and water in the desert. They were so impatient with him that they threatened to stone him if they did not get what they wanted.

> *"The whole Israelite community set out from the Desert of Sin, traveling from place to place as the Lord had commanded. They camped at Rephidim, but there was no water for the people to drink. So they quarreled with Moses and said, "Give us water to drink." Moses replied, "Why do you quarrel with me? Why do you put the Lord to the test?"*
>
> *But the people were thirsty for water there, and they grumbled against*
>
> *Moses. They said, "Why did you bring us up out of Egypt to make us and our children and livestock die of thirst?" Then Moses cried to the Lord, "What am I to do with these people? They are almost ready to stone me."*
> (Exodus 17:1–4)

It is easy to judge them as people of little faith, but it is important to remember the context and the environment where they were; the desert is no oasis. They were crossing a barren, desiccated, hyper-arid area in a region that is known today to have an average annual precipitation of just four to five millimeters. Consequently, dehydration was a major concern for everyone, particularly, the elderly and children. In addition, the heat and the lack of vegetation exposed the surface of the ground to denudation, which resulted in difficulty feeding even the livestock. Sidebothan, in his book "The Red Land" stated:

> Any human living in the Eastern Desert had to learn very quickly how to find, protect, store and distribute water in the most careful and efficient manner possible.[1]

1. Steven E. Sidebothan, Martin Hence, and Hendrikje M Nouwens, *The Red Land: The Illustrated Archaeology of Egypt's Eastern Desert* (Cairo: The American University in Cairo Press 2008), 26.

We should also mention the natural dangers of the desert: sandstorms, scorpions, deadly snakes, contaminated water, etc. The mere thought of three days in such a landscape is enough to trigger fear, depression, and anxiety. To better understand the risks of the desert, Numbers 21:4–6 says:

> The people grew impatient on the way; they spoke against God and against Moses, and said, "Why have you brought us up out of Egypt to die in the wilderness? There is no bread! There is no water! and we detest this miserable food!"

The food they so detested was the mana that God had provided them. For a moment, the Lord removed his protective shield and the snakes that once were running away from them now are attacking and biting them. The end of verse 6 says: "Many Israelites died."

The environment was not conducive; they were former slaves (about two million) who had never known freedom, who were used to having masters providing them with pots of meat, and all the food they wanted. (Ex. 16:3). So, three days into their journey, when their reserve of water was exhausted, they were at "Mara" (bitterness), they grumbled against their leader; God responded and gave them water. The pressure was on Moses; they depended on him for everything: from settling disagreements, providing them with food and water, to directions to the promised land. The book of Numbers tells us that Moses heard the people of every family *wailing* as they are going to their tents. They were complaining and stood in opposition to everything God ordered him to do until he cried out to the Lord in verse 14 of Numbers 11:

> "I cannot carry all these people by myself; the burden is too heavy for me. If this is how you are going to treat me, please go ahead and kill me — if I have found favor in your eyes—and do not let me face my ruin." (Numbers 11:14,15)

The Bible tells of other persons who have known great deal of pain; Paul can be an example. In second Corinthians eleven, beginning in verse twenty-four, we have the autobiography of a man who is in constant danger.

> "Five times I received from the Jews the forty lashes minus one. Three times I was beaten with rods, once I was pelted with stones, three times I was shipwrecked, I spent a night and a day in the open sea, I have been constantly on the move. I have been in danger from rivers, in danger from bandits, in danger from my fellow Jews, in danger from Gentiles; in danger in the city, in danger in the country, in danger at sea; and in danger from false believers. I have labored and toiled and have often gone without sleep; I have known hunger and thirst and have often gone without food; I have been cold and naked." (2 Cor. 11: 24–27)

In this short paragraph, he has recorded being in danger eight times. More than once, he has been beaten, chained, and imprisoned for the sake of the Gospel; he could have easily blamed God for allowing him to have known so much pain. Yet, he continued his ministry of encouragement. To the Philippians he said to rejoice "always" in the Lord, to the Romans and the Corinthians, he said nothing can separate me from the love of God manifested in Jesus Christ.

> "We are pressed on every side but not crushed; perplexed, but not in despair; persecuted, but not abandoned; struck down, but not destroyed." (2 Cor. 4: 8–9)

He concluded the chapter in a seemingly masochist tone:

> "I delight in weaknesses, in insults, in hardships, in persecutions, in difficulties. For when I am weak, then I am strong." (2 Cor 2:10)

Another person who did not seem to have been affected by despair is David. God promised this boy a kingdom when he was in his teens; he was anointed by Samuel the prophet and was waiting to be crown king. Before that was to happen however, he had to live the most difficult chapter of his life.

He was running from cave to cave, facing hunger and thirst from Saul who was determined to kill him. Nothing was stopping him, even sacred ground; the prophet's house was not exempted. He made several attempts to personally kill him, and when he failed, he hired professional killers to assassinate him in his wife's bedroom if necessary. David was completely frustrated when he realized that these murderers were old friends from the army, people he had fought shoulder to shoulder with. In Ps. 59:5, he called them "wicked traitors." In one of his poems, he stated:

> "My heart is anguished within me; the terrors of death assail me. Fear and trembling have beset me; horror has overwhelmed me." (Ps 55:4, 5)

The amazing thing about this man is that: every time he seems to be at the border of hopelessness, he always finds comfort in the justice and the protection of the Lord. In the same Psalm 59 where he made the case against those "traitors" who were setting traps to kill him, he concluded the Psalms with verse sixteen where it says:

> "But I will sing of your strength, in the morning I will sing of your love; for you are my fortress, my refuge in times of trouble. You are my strength, I sing praise to you; you, God, are my fortress, my God on whom I can rely." (Ps 59:16, 17)

His confidence in the Lord was resolute. He was determined to not let the circumstances he was facing affect his reliance on God. Indeed, fear and faith can coexist. David, while running from Saul, fled to Gath, the city of Goliath whom he had recently killed. When he was found out, the servants of the king said to him:

> "Isn't this David, the king of the land? Isn't he the one they sing about in their dances: "Saul has slain his thousands, and David his tens of thousands"?" David took these words to heart and was very much afraid of Achish king of Gath. So, he pretended to be insane in their presence; and while he was in their hands he acted like a madman, making marks on doors of the gate and letting saliva run down his beard. Achish said to his servants,

"Look at the man! He is insane! Why bring him to me?"
(1 Sam 21:11–14)

David looked at this mob that was about to take his life, and fear overtook him. The fear was pulling him down violently to despair when faith as a solace came to his rescue.

> "When I am afraid, I put my trust in you. In God, whose word I praise—in God I trust and I am not afraid. What can mere mortals do to me?" (Ps 56:3, 4)

Right after that, his instinct reminded him of self-preservation and he was faced with doubt, he said:

> "All day long they twist my words; all their schemes are for my ruin. They conspire, they lurk, and they watch my steps, hoping to take my life." (Ps 56:5, 6)

There was a fierce battle in his mind between faith and hopelessness and he began verse five with the realization that he was indeed "walking in the valley of death."

Like in any battle, the enemy never puts down his weapon and never surrenders without a fight. The battle of the mind is what the enemy rages war against in every Christian's life; it is the center of command. If he is allowed to take control of it, the war is over. This cloud of doubt and fear was about to blind David, he was like someone who was drowning and in desperate need of air. Faith came to his rescue like someone coming up from under the water to get a puff of air; faith overpowered that fear. David concluded the Psalm with complete confidence in God by saying:

> "For you have delivered me from death and my feet from stumbling, that I may walk before God in the light of life." (Psalm 56:13)

These are just a few of the many people in the Bible that have been terribly affected by the power of depression while in ministry, but praise be to God that in every one of those examples, despair was never able to stand toe to toe against the hope of eternity.

DISCUSSION QUESTIONS

1. Is your back against the wall? Are you feeling conquered?

_____

_____

_____

2. How did you make it this far? Where did you get help from?

_____

_____

_____

3. Are you feeling in a state of despair? Can you put this in words?

_____

_____

_____

4. Have you talked to anyone about it?

_____

_____

_____

5. Who or what is your adversary? Is it fear, doubt or the uncertainty of tomorrow?

_____

_____

_____

WORTHLESSNESS

Martin Luther King states in a famous speech that: The value of a person resides in the content of his character. We have learned to appreciate a person based on his/her ability to produce, to be useful to us when we need them. Likewise, we consider ourselves valuable when we feel important and necessary in the environment we are thriving. Normally, we do not save things we don't need, neither do we waste time with someone that has nothing to offer. Employers are always searching for the best fit for his company and he/she most likely will not hire a prospective engineer before graduation. The term worthlessness can be deceiving without an understanding of the environment. We don't need a mechanic in an art studio, no matter how great a mechanic he is; likewise, an accomplished surgeon is worthless on a construction site. In Exodus 35, we read that God, in the building of his tabernacle, ordered Moses to select people He had previously gifted with the Spirit of God, with wisdom, understanding and knowledge.

> "Then Moses said to the Israelites, "See, the Lord has chosen Bezalel son of Uri, the son of Hur, of the tribe of Judah, and he has filled him with the Spirit of God, with wisdom, with understanding, with knowledge and with all kinds of skills—to make artistic designs for work in gold, silver and bronze, to cut and set stones, to engage in all kinds of artistic crafts. He has filled them with skill to do all kinds of work as engravers, designers, embroiders in blue, purple and scarlet yarn and fine linen, and weavers—all of them skilled workers and designers." (Exodus 35: 30–33, 35)

Bezalel, who was an artist and sculptor was an important asset in the construction of the tabernacle; but he would have been worthless if Moses had put an ephod on him and placed him among the priests. Someone can be considered worthless solely by the method or the person doing the evaluation. Even our garbage is a treasure for someone else.

Anyone who is despised, hated, in a house or a workplace by a group of people, may be loved and precious to someone else. That person who is about to be executed for being "a threat" for others is someone else's best friend, or husband. A man's life can mean nothing to one but a precious gift for someone else.

You may be disgusted and sickened by the presence of someone in your company; but who are we to say that he/she is worthless. Maybe you are perfectly comfortable with that attitude since it is shared by most of your coworkers. He/she is labeled as: worthless, no one values his/her opinion; in fact, he/she is made completely insignificant. He/she failed many of his/her projects, rarely talks to anybody, he is always sad and depressed, on the verge of being fired. He lives alone and seems to be completely consumed by the job, trying to be accepted. He/she is finally convinced of his worthlessness and secretly begins to entertain suicidal thoughts. This poor person is literally being tortured in that job; he/she is now convinced that he/she is "useless," "*nobody needs me.*" Is it true? Can someone created in God's image be really worthless? Well, let's look at the Bible. In the book of Proverbs, we read:

> "The purposes of a person's heart are deep waters, but
> one who has insight draws them out." (Proverbs 20:5)

Someone who seems to have a lack of understanding may possibly be living far from his purpose. He/she may be working very hard trying to be productive in one particular environment but always falls short. The reason is not worthlessness; to the contrary, it is primarily because he hasn't discovered his true potential or he/she is being evaluated by someone with no insight. Because of lack of discernment, evaluators have labeled inconsequential many great minds. Every human being made in God's image has hidden purposes, and it takes a person with insight to decode them. God confirmed that in the book of Jeremiah when he said:

> "For I know the plans I have for you," declares the Lord."
> (Jeremiah 29:11)

Emphasis here is on the personal pronoun; God said *I* know the plans. Everyone would agree that the will of God is not revealed to everyone. In Genesis 18:17, God was about to destroy Sodom and Gomorrah, but he did not tell everybody or even the citizens of the city. He only talked to his friend Abraham and said: "*Shall I hide from Abraham what I am about to do?*" There is a sense of guilt in that sentence. God feels that he cannot do something like that without telling his good friend. So, God only reveals his heart to those who have intimacy with him. People may have purposes for which they were created that are unknown to them and others because they do not seek the face and will of God. So, worthlessness is not a quality in God's creation; everyone is valuable, and important in one way or the other. Jesus confirms that in Matthew 25. The parable says that each servant was entrusted with talents; some more than others but they all had something. How, when and if we are going to use the talent is a decision we have to make but the master entrusts everyone with at least one.

DEPRESSION AND RELIGIOUS LEADERS

Depression is a stigma that enters any community without regard for the person or status. When it wraps its tentacles around someone, it shows no mercy. Not only does it suck joy out of its victims, it also negatively affects others around them. Everyone is aware of its destructive power and are desperately searching of some sort of remedy. Some seek medical help which often are inadequate in providing lasting results, others pursue counseling. What needs to be remembered is that the medical community has not been able to provide consistent results[1] in response to that dilemma. The moment has come for the world to explore other options.

Many Christians prefer to go to their pastors or a Christian counselor for help when they are depressed. They figure that since clergymen are licensed to teach about God, they must be qualified and equipped to counsel and advise a depressed soul. So during times of anxiety, members of a congregation strongly believe the pastor to be the primary source of help, the "superman" to visit. How true is this proposition? A study published in churchleaders.com seems to present a rebuttal to this conjecture. Megan Briggs, editor for Churchleaders.com published a study that was conducted by Rev. Andrew Irvine from Knox College of the University of Toronto. In 338 responses from a survey[2] gathered among ministers of some Protestant denominations, he found:

1. Frank et al., *Archives.*

2. Megan Briggs, "Why are Pastors Depressed? A look at the research," September 23, 2019, CHURCHLEADERS.COM, https://churchleaders.com/news/359562-why-are-pastors-depressed-a-look-at-the-research.html.

70 percent moderately or strongly disagreed with the statement, "I feel fulfilled in ministry."

67 percent strongly agreed with the statement, "I sometimes project my job frustration on the family."

62 percent strongly agreed with the statement, "Sometimes my outward

appearance seems happy and content while inside I am emotionally distressed."

75 percent strongly agreed with the statement, "I am afraid to let my parishioners know how I really feel."

He started his report by saying how evangelical churches are beginning to be aware of the fact that many of their pastors are struggling with mental illness, including depression and suicidal thoughts. In the same report, he further stated that 18% could not identify one single close friend, 55% said that they feel sometimes very lonely and 16% said that they have been diagnosed with depression.

He is not alone; in case you were to doubt this report, let's look further. Some statistics compiled by sources like Global Pastors Network, Pastor to Pastor and others seem to support that finding. In fact, this is not recent; it has been like that for years. In the September/October 2000 edition of *Physician Magazine*, Dr. Walt Larimore, who formally was vice president of medical outreach at Focus on the Family, and Rev. Bill Peel reported surveys indicating 80% of pastors and 84% of their spouses are discouraged or are dealing with depression. In addition, more than 40% of pastors and 47% of their spouses report that they are suffering from burnout.

A letter from a Pastor to another fellow pastor reads like this:

Dear Pastor and People,
I am at a place in ministry where I feel depressed and devoid of any desire to do ministry. How can I get help and still be effective in ministry? I feel like I am losing hope but have to act like everything is ok with my

fellow brothers in ministry. They just have a get over it attitude.

Jeffrey

Furthermore, Dr. R. C. Sproul in one of his monthly articles titled: "The Dark Night of the Soul." He describes the phenomenon as:

Depression then can become a medical problem if the soul is left starving for too long

The malady that provoked David to soak his pillow with tears. It was the malady that earned for Jeremiah the sobriquet, "The Weeping Prophet." It was the malady that so afflicted Martin Luther that his melancholy threatened to destroy him. ... It is a depression that is linked to a crisis of faith, a crisis that comes when one senses the absence of God or gives rise to a feeling of abandonment by Him.[3]

It is important to remember that pastors are also creatures with emotions and needs, they are subject to loneliness and depression; this is the norm. Paul however in his letter to the Philippians disregards this reality and ordered Christians to "*Always Rejoice*" (Phil. 4:4). In the midst of so much evidence, should we just reject Paul's request and face the reality? How do Christians define depression?

1. Some say that it is the inability to love oneself.

2. Others claim it is a medical problem.

3. Or not trusting God.

4. Yet others, say it is the result of demonic activity that oppresses the soul.

To answer these propositions, we are going to begin by explaining the phenomenon of a Grumbling Soul. Jesus was talking to Satan on the mountain during the temptation when he said:

3. R.C. Sproul, "Spiritual Depression: The Dark Night of The Soul," in *Tabletalk Magazine*, August 7, 2019, https://www.ligonier.org/blog/the-dark-night-of-the-soul/.

"Man does not live by bread alone, but by every word that pro-
ceeds out of the mouth of God." (Matthew 4:4)

In 1 Thessalonians 5:23, Paul tells us that man is "tripartite"
(body, mind, and spirit). Each unit is different and yet interrelated.
God created them for different reasons and also they must be nurtured, fed, and cared for differently. Here in Matthew 4, Jesus is
saying that man should be tuned to listen to the hungry sound
of each unit. It is understood that no one can hear the sound of
a hungry soul in the same way that he would hear the grumbling
of a stomach, but both make a sound that can be described and
understood.

Hungry Stomach

The stomach can be very loud; when it is empty and needs of your
attention, you would know. It then produces hormones that causes
the brain to reply by signaling the digestive muscles to begin
contracting; this contraction is called "peristalsis." It also signals
the brain to stimulate the stomach and the intestines to secrete
digestive juices. So, the noise that we are accustomed to respond
to so quickly is the result of contractions which cause movement
of gas and fluid between the stomach and the small intestines. This
muscular organ is conditioned by God to behave in this manner
for the wellbeing of the entire body; when it growls, we jump. We
speak and understand its language, and never do we let its calls go
unanswered. Some people are so punctual in fulfilling this task,
that they become proactive to the point of addiction. Doctors, di-
etitians, and therapists now must train people to not overfeed the
stomach. The same teaching is also extended to children, so they
do not neglect the grumbling of a stomach. It is one of the necessi-
ties of life beside shelter and clothing of course; a modern list also
includes education.

Hungry Mind

As creatures made in God's image, we are advised to train our minds in the knowledge of his creation. God, the prime instructor, initiated the first lesson in the book of Psalms, the chapter 19:1:

> "The heavens declare the glory of God; the skies proclaim the works of his hands."

His instructions are not limited in the understanding of planets, galaxies, and constellations. He also encourages the wise to add to their learning, to gain wisdom rather than gold, and insight rather than silver. (Proverbs 16:16) Why seek wisdom over gold? Everyone knows that gold and silver are well known commodities that are used as medium of exchange, they control the actions and motivations of many. But in Rom. 3:4 we read:

> "Let God be true and every human being a liar."

If the Bible claims that wisdom is better than gold, then wisdom must be a possible currency that can be used to acquire gold.

People often say that wisdom can generate money but not vice versa. Rather its presence is expressed in terms of experience, knowledge, and good judgement. Wisdom is an abstract concept that cannot be seen, touched, smelled, or heard; many equate it with the number of credentials after someone's name. When a person is gifted with knowledge, that possession comes with respect, appreciation, and particularly a good position in society; the thirst for knowledge is palpable. The potential reward that is attached to it causes a continual increase in the price of educational institutions. Knowledge is sought with a passion because it is *the key to freedom.* Even the government gets involved; it mandates that parents educate their children or pay a hefty price. If an empty mind doesn't make noise to get our attention, the isolation and humiliation that it attracts get us motivated.

Hungry Soul

The world is experiencing one of the worst drought of its existence. That drought doesn't affect vegetation and animals in the wild, but the heart and soul of man. It causes people to lose their mind, abandon their own family, fall into addiction and other drastic activities out of desperation for anything that resembles water. Those resemblances unfortunately are only mirages, optical illusions in a hot desert; they have no capacity to quench thirst. The culture is continuously pushing substitutes that apparently seem to offer relief to a thirsty soul but in reality they only magnify the desire and leave the person empty. The soul can be thirsty and hungry for generations and remain undetected, not because of lack of signs but discernment. You see, a body has many different parts that require attention, but the soul is the most neglected; its subtle and silent character contributes to its abandonment and suffering. Christians would rather medicate the soul to drowsiness than to seek understanding that would help to adequately feed it. In third John 1:2 the Bible says:

> "Beloved, I pray that in all respects you may prosper and be in good health, just as your soul prospers."

This verse summarizes God's intentions for his servants. To him, spiritual growth should be the most important principal in their lives; he wants it to be the guide in the search for completeness. He certainly values good health and prosperity, but not to the same extent as the soul. He wants prosperity of the soul to be the guide for the rest of the body. So, when it comes to food, we should be more concerned with the soul than with the body and the mind. Jesus said to Satan that "*man does not live by bread alone*." As materialists, we tend to be concerned about the apparent and the obvious. Jesus is fully God and man, He understands that. In fact, the purpose of his coming was to teach human how to live a fulfilled life without compromising their relation with God (Heb. 4:15). *Alone* means that it is okay to care for the flesh without neglecting the needs of the other two. It is also worth remembering that Jesus has deprived the body of food for forty days and nights.

At this point, the crave for nourishment is extreme and the enemy knows that for he came as an advocate for that flesh, begging the master to feed it; he cannot tolerate a weak flesh particularly when the spirit is being well fed. His job hasn't changed, he still stands as the greatest promoter of the flesh advising the believer to go on indulging in sin. He knew that Jesus' action was uncommon to mankind and he asked him to turn rock into bread to stop it; but his offer was rejected. Materialism causes us to see life on one level; so, he spoke for the materialists. The priority is made clear in John 1:2; here he is responding as a rebuke to the way we are living. *Man should not live by bread alone!* When people wake up in the morning, they don't wait for the stomach to begin rumbling before they take breakfast. On the contrary, they set a time to eat before going to work. If the stomach must grumble for the food, it is because the mealtime has already passed. Likewise, feeding the soul should take place at a specific time in the morning; if it has to rumble, it is already late.

The stomach is very talkative. It doesn't care if you are in a church, a conference hall or in the company of your girl/boyfriend; if it needs to be fed, it will be loud enough to be heard across the room. The soul is just the opposite; even when it is desperately in need, its cry is still very delicate and soft. You must be tuned to listen to its cry. If you are too busy with life, you can easily misinterpret that cry for something else and as a result provide a cure that causes more damage than good.

Nourishing the Soul

The Bible tells us in Genesis 2:7 that *God made man from dust of the ground*; after creation, the mannequin laid lifeless in front of him. Then *God breathed into his nostrils the breath of life.* The verse ends by saying that: *The man became a living being.*

Science tells us that there are three kinds of animals: terrestrial, aquatic, and amphibian. Each category finds its nourishment in the environment where it was created to survive. Dogs in the wild for example do not find their food in water nor do fish on the land. Even without a mother, a baby animal can survive in its environment if no predator eats it. In Genesis 1:26–28, God gave to mankind dominion over all creation including the three categories: terrestrial, aquatic, and amphibian; in Chapter 9:3, he gave them the right to eat meat. It means that the body that was made with material would have found fulfillment in that material from which it was created if God did not have to blow life into its nostrils. If he had chosen another means to give life to that mass other than his own breath, man would have been fully satisfied with just the material. He did not do that; as an artist, he felt that it was necessary to sign his work. He felt that it was important to make an investment in his creation and he did. That investment put a permanent twist in the needs of man. God with one breath poured his complete attribute into man. Never can their needs be solely material; it is fully divine and fully terrestrial.

There is no secret in nourishing the soul. The soul is a person, he can rejoice or suffer, he has features and can eat; it indwells the personality. *My soul rejoices in the Lord.* (Ps. 103:1) The body is the habitation of the soul and the spirit. Without Christ, a person is dead spiritually; he/she is carrying around a dead body. When the person is born again, Jesus comes into the spirit as the word and brings life. *He is formed in the spirit* (Gal. 4:19) and the spirit is now alive and needs nourishment. Psalm 119:93, says that *I am quickened with the word.* When the believer reads or hears the word, it goes through the ear, down to the soul where it is meditated on (the soul ponders and thinks about what is read); the digestion is done in the soul. The soulish feeds the spirit which sucks the word in for survival. The spirit, being from God, only feeds on the word of God. Once the word gets into the spirit, it becomes powerful; the spirit of God energizes it and makes it powerful. Matthew 12:34 says that: *Out of the abundance of the heart the mouth speaketh.* When the word comes out of the mouth of the believer, it comes as power; it goes in as *Logos* and comes out as *Rema.* The Spirit of God transforms it into *Rema.* An abundance of that power in the soul will eventually manifest in the physical body. When power is overflowing in the spirit, it kicks back to the soul and comes out through the mouth of the believer as power. Conversely, when the word is not meditated on, it goes in through the ears and out through the mouth with no power (it comes in as word and out as word)

The necessity for the believer to allow his spirit to quicken the word is paramount. He must be acute to listening because the enemy is on the lookout to provide believers with counterfeit nourishment to appease their soul. There is no materialistic nourishment for the soul; it is spiritual and must be provided with spiritual food. Meditating means thinking about what is read; it is feeding the soul, the source of joy.

Soul Expression

It is understood that we cannot hear the sound of a hungry soul as we would the sound of a stomach. The stomach is not timid, it has no shame or fear asking for help and it is persistent. The soul on the other hand, expresses its needs through feelings of loneliness, despair, emptiness, or some desire that we don't quite understand; we call it: depression. In other words, depression is an expression of the soul, a natural reaction of the body for some unknown. The spirit comes from God, and the soul which houses man's personality cannot live independently from the spirit. Jean Jacques Rousseau in his discourse on arts and sciences says that: *Man is naturally born good and happy, it is society that corrupts him.* We should instead say that man is in a constant conflict between the original sin that he inherited from Adam and the personality that he gets from God. The book of Matthew talks of a man who once asked Jesus:

> "Teacher, what must I do to have eternal life?"
> Jesus replied, "You shall not murder, you shall not commit adultery, you shall not steal, you shall not give false testimony, honor your father and mother and love your neighbor as yourself." (Matthew 19:18, 19)

We often find people who do not follow Christ but have good morals and flee from evil.

God is heavenly, therefore nourishment for that soul must come from God. The Bible said in John 4 that Jesus had not eaten for a long time and the disciples were pressing him to eat and he said unto them that *he has food to eat that they know nothing about... his food is to do the will of his father and to finish his works.* So, the food for the soul is not terrestrial, aquatic or amphibian; it is heavenly. Just like the body, the soul can be hungry but the way it expresses that hunger is unknown to man. Since we only operate on one wavelength, we have no idea how to interpret that sound, we give it a materialistic interpretation; we call it depression and many professionals are ready to give it a seal of approval. When the soul is left starving for too long, its cry becomes desperate and that extended exposure can indeed create a sense of depression that requires medical attention.

Satan does not initiate depression; he only uses it as a tool to bring Christians down. When the soul is starving for the Bread of Life and other forms of solution are sought to calm it, he takes this opportunity to create doubt in the mind: *Nobody loves you, you are a failure, nobody cares about you, all your effort means nothing,* etc. The pressure can be so overwhelming that it creates a sense of hopelessness; the only alternative is suicide. Depression is one of the best tools in the hand of the enemy and he knows how to use it.

Furthermore, it is not "demonic activity in the soul" as many believe -- When someone becomes a child of God, the Holy Spirit makes his dwelling in him and he does not share houses with demons. Should we say that depression is an exclusivity of the secular? Not at all, because many great men of God were affected by it. David was not possessed. In Psalm 55 he says:

> "My heart is in anguish within me; the terrors of death assail me. Fear and trembling have beset me; horror has overwhelmed me." (verses 4, 5)

Jesus on the Mount of Olives was also "anguished." This word translates as "distressed, sorrowful."

And being in anguish, he prayed more earnestly, and his sweat was like drops of blood falling on the ground. (Luke 22:44)

Jesus was fighting the flesh; he knew the reason he came (Revelation 13:8). *The lamb that was slain before the foundation of the world.* The time now has come, and the flesh says no. In verse 42 he says: "*Father, if you are willing, take this cup away from me.*" He saw the pain that he had to endure and wanted to back up. *An angel from heaven appeared and strengthened him.* He needed strength because he was facing the biggest challenge of his life and he could not back up because of his obedience; even the Father, his eternal partner, had left him. He was suffering a temporary loss of fellowship with God the Father.

If depression is a thirst or hunger for the bread of Life, how can religious leaders be depressed since they are always versed in the word of God?

The answer is simple. Pastors and their wives are too busy feeding the flock that they have little or no time to care for themselves and their family. When they hear a good sermon, instead of hearing God talking to them, they take notes so they can re-preach it to their congregations. To give life, you must have life; one cannot save someone from death if he/she is dead. Jesus said to Peter that Satan has asked to sift them as wheat (Peter and the other disciples); he promised to pray for him to be strong so he can strengthen the others. Jesus offered to save Peter so in turn, he can save others. One of the Federal Aviation Administration advisories to airlines states that:

> "The ability to take corrective and protective action is lost in 20 to 30 minutes at 18,000 feet and 5 to 12 minutes at 20,000 feet, followed soon thereafter by unconsciousness."[4]

4. Liz Neporent, "What Happens When a Plane's Cabin Depressurized Loss of cabin pressure triggers confusion before sleepiness and even death," September 5, 2014, abcnews.go.com, https://abcnews.go.com/Health/planes-cabin-depressurizes/story?id=25277752.

Let's say you are on a commercial flight at 35000 feet with a child and the cabin air pressure is beginning to drop; the FAA would want you to first put on your oxygen mask before helping the child with his/hers. The reason is that if you care for the child first, you might lose consciousness before having the time to care for yourself. This is exactly what Jesus is trying to teach Peter; pastors and their family should be well fed so they can be strong enough to feed the sheep. Sometimes they are so busy spoon-feeding the flock that they forget their own; when they finally turn their attention to home, it is too late; the enemy has already destroyed it.

In Luke 22:32, Jesus told Peter of Satan's scheme to destroy them but he prayed for his restoration and asked him to care for his brothers thereafter. Similarly, a pastor needs time to replenish so his ministry can be effective. It is not wise for a Pastor to run every committee in the church along with a full-time ministry. It is not possible to be preaching two messages on Sunday, teach Sunday school, do announcements, be present in every meeting, do counseling, home visits etc ...There is no time left to run his own home, discipline his children and be a good father/husband. Study shows that many of their wives are also depressed because they are being dragged in this superhuman lifestyle in private while they must keep a smiley, happy face in public. There is no time to replenish. One advising Pastor sent an answer to another fellow Pastor who was considering giving up ministry that reads like this:

> Dear Jeffrey,
>
> Your situation is the same as numerous pastors around the world. You feel as if you are ineffective in ministry because of your current state of mind and heart. You give and give and never get anything back. I know, I have been in the same exact place.
>
> I would suggest first, to take a small break. Take a few weeks off from your pastoral and ministry duties. You are not quitting on God but simply refueling yourself. Sit under good preaching and teaching during this break. Go outdoors and enjoy God's creation as you read, pray, and refocus your thoughts upon His glory and call upon your life.

Your fellow brothers in ministry who feel as if you need to "get over it" do not understand the problem of pastoral depression and emptiness but will before their ministry is over. Seek the counsel of a wise older pastor who has been in the ministry for many years. Someone who understands what you are going through.

Unfortunately this is not a quick fix and one that will take much prayer, discipline, and devotion on your part. I pray you rise forth from this valley soon

Dustin

DISCUSSION QUESTIONS

1. Are you a Pastor or Religious Leader?

_____

_____

2. Is depression a major issue in your life? How?

_____

_____

3. If you are a Pastor, do you have a mentor? Have you ever felt like giving up ministry? Who do you share that with?

_____

_____

4. Are your kids seeing you as their pastor or their dad?

_____

_____

5. How often do you take quality time with your wife, away from ministry?

_____

_____

6. Have you allowed Jesus to awaken your spirit?

_____

_____

7. What does it mean to meditate on the word?

_____

_____

ELDERS

The previous chapter described pastoring as a difficult field where people can be stressed and exhausted, where families can be neglected, and careers held by a thread. Before we even consider the reasons for such a grim statistic, there is one reality that needs to be said: *Jesus Christ is the Great High Priest* (Heb.4:11); as such, he is the one who chooses his ministers.

> "So Christ himself gave the apostles, the prophets, the evangelists, the pastors and teachers, to equip his people for works of service.." (Eph. 4:11,12a)

Those who get into ministry without a call, come with their own agenda; they don't have a desire to serve. They easily get tired, disappointed, and sometimes just leave when the going gets tough. There are others that are called, they serve to exhaustion like Moses and soon get overwhelmed. Every worker must have a time of rest lest he faints or deliver a very sloppy job; God worked for six days and rested the seventh. If someone were given a load to carry up a mountain for some distance and he decided to go non-stop, even with a good attitude, he would either collapse or give up before the end. Conversely, if he is encouraged, allowed to rest, eat, and drink, he would gain energy and would be able to carry on to destination. Similarly, a pastor is like a battery that is constantly giving out energy; preach, teach, counsel, respond to emergency calls, do visits, etc. He/she needs to be allowed to stop giving so he can receive. He/she needs to have time to refresh; to be ministered to. He is a human with a soul that needs to be fed lest he (soul) becomes malnourished and eventually depressed and devoid of any desire to continue carrying the load. A pastor needs the love and encouragement of his parishioners.

Jesus the great instructor taught us that lesson. In Luke 22, when he realized that the work ahead was too heavy for him; he wanted to give up.

> Jesus went out as usual to the Mount of Olives and the disciples followed him. On reaching the place, he said to them, "Pray that you do not fall into temptation." He withdrew about a stone's throw beyond them, knelt down and prayed, "Father, if you are willing, take this cup from me; yet not my will, but yours be done." An angel from God appeared to him and strengthened him. And being "in anguish," he prayed more earnestly, and his sweat was like drops of blood falling to the ground. (Verses 39–44)

It was customary for Jesus to come to the mountain to converse with his Father; this time however, it was different. Humanly speaking, he looked at the work ahead and wanted to give up. *Father, if you are willing, take this cup away from me.* Jesus envisioned the agony and the pain that awaited him, and he wanted to back up. He responded however, using Psalm 9:9: *The Lord is a shelter for the oppressed, a refuge in times of trouble.* When distress and torment were stronger, he prayed more earnestly. This is a very practical example for a Christian in difficult times. There are many reasons for a pastor to feel abandoned, misunderstood, overlooked, hated, overworked, distressed, even persecuted. This is a perfect time to go to the mountain alone and replenish, to nourish the soul; an angel came to strengthen Jesus. When Joshua was taking the role of Moses, God said to him:

> As I was with Moses, so I will be with you; I will never leave you nor forsake you. *Be strong and courageous…* (Joshua 1:5b, 6a)

Those that are called need to remember the promise: that they will never be forsaken. Furthermore, Paul left us the example of a very accomplished ministry through suffering. 2 Corinthians 4: 8–11 states:

> We are hard pressed on every side, but not crushed; perplexed, but not in despair, persecuted, but not abandoned; struck down, but not destroyed. We always carry around the death of Jesus, so that the life of Jesus may also be revealed in our body. For we who are alive are always being given over to death for Jesus' sake, so that his life may be revealed in our mortal body.

Often, when we look at the many problems facing our lives, and the little time we have to solve them, we feel justified in our discouragement. However, when we remember that the Lord does not need a bridge to get us to the other side, we are thrilled with excitement in the midst of the problems.

DISCUSSION QUESTIONS

1. Are you involved in ministry? Are you a pastor, a Sunday school teacher, in children's ministry?

   _____

   _____

2. Do you ever feel overwhelmed and misunderstood as a religious leader? Do you ever feel like giving up? What keeps you going?

   _____

   _____

3. Do you use some kind of "Get over it attitude" to keep you going?

   _____

   _____

4. Is there something to learn from Jesus or Paul in relation to anguish?

_____

_____

5. What do you do to replenish your soul?

_____

_____

BE TUNED TO LISTEN!

"I spread out my hands to you, my soul thirsts

for you like a parched land."

—PSALM 143:6

In a previous chapter, we explained the phenomenon of a grumbling stomach; the audible sound that it produces quickly reminds us that *we need bread*. Besides the sensation that is created in the hypothalamus, the ears are tuned to listen, interpret and act on the sounds coming from the body. Cars also are maintained the same way; the more you know its functioning, the more you will understand the source of a noise and its meaning. Similarly, we have little tolerance for pain; when we have a headache, we don't wait; we rapidly reach for a Tylenol or some other pain reliever. Being able to understand your body is a sign of maturity; a medical professional depends on the patient's explanation of his pains to write a prescription.

Physical hunger, pain sensation, and the coding of a computer are all different forms of language that require patience to understand; we have conquered them. A mother normally takes time to understand the language of her newborn; the pitch of the baby's cry means different things to a mother than it does to a complete stranger. Some people with persistence have even penetrated things in nature: the bark of a dog, the hiss of a snake, etc.

If we can accomplish so much with things that are temporal, then certainly if we tune our mind to listening to the soul, we will be able to comprehend and satisfy its needs. In Psalm 143:6 we read:

> I spread out my hands to you, my soul thirsts for you like a parched land.

The grumbling of the soul is comparable to a parched land; it is silent. It is a deceptive silence that lets you believe that all is well until it is so dry and desolated that it splits open. The mind must be acutely tuned to listen to be able to perceive the cry of the soul. It is very subtle; it can remain undetected for a long time while major damages are taking place. The enemy often uses it to cause the downfall of many. Jesus encountered him on the mountain after his baptism.

In Matthew chapter 4 we read that Jesus went on the mountain and fasted for forty days and nights feeding his soul with the presence of the Lord; he was physically hungry. Satan, knowing that his body should be crying for attention, tried to tell him that the voice that he hears in his subconscious was in fact his body, not the soul. You should *"Tell these stones to become bread"* to satisfy your hunger. Well, Jesus was really hungry; after spending forty days and night fasting, he needed food. Instead of performing the miracle to make bread to satisfy his needs, he took the opportunity to teach a lesson.

In this dialogue, Satan was trying to play the same card he has often played many times against believers. It seems that he was trying to help the master: *You have been taking care of the soul for forty days, it is about time you turn your attention to the flesh. The cry that brought you here in the first place wasn't that of an hungry soul; to the contrary, it was a regular, normal physical need: the body needs bread.* He even questioned the Lord's identity, asking him to prove that he was the Son of God: *If you are the Son of God...* turn these stones into bread to satisfy your hunger. Jesus' answer was somewhat of an organizational lesson: there is a time for everything; a time for the soul, a time for the stomach. *Man does not live by bread alone.*

Satan didn't give up, he took Jesus to the top of the mountain (verse 9) *okay, you didn't need bread; you miss your glory, the glory you had with your father.* He offered him *all the kingdoms of the world and their splendor in exchange for Christ's worship.* This weapon is one of the deadliest in his arsenal; he has been using it for years to bring high towers down crumbling: *The feeling of loneliness, that sadness, that sense of depression that you have is in fact a desire for power and authority; do not confuse that for something spiritual. It is a desire to dominate, to be great, to shine. It is not your soul that needs to be fed, it is your pride. Worship me and I will return to you the kingdom that you have left and you won't have to endure the cross.* Fortunately, Jesus knew the sound of the soul and would not confuse it for something else; he rebuked the enemy.

> "The sinful nature desires what is contrary to the Spirit."
> (Galatians 5:17)

> "Get away Satan! It is written: worship the Lord your
> God and serve him only." (Matthew 4:10)

This encounter is common to Christians; it takes place almost daily with one difference: the outcome is not always the same. Many believers often mistake the desires of the soul for material needs so when the soul speaks, they respond with the material. The soul expresses its hunger through sadness, feeling of emptiness, sense of depression, etc. If we are not tuned to listen and comprehend the language, before we even attempt to decode the sounds, the enemy is already in our face with a tray of materials. When the materials he offers do not fill the void, he offers a new one. There is no substitute for praising the Lord; drugs or medical interventions are often ineffective. The French philosopher Blaise Pascal puts it this way:

> "There is a God-shaped vacuum in the heart of every
> man which cannot be filled by any created thing, but
> only by God, the Creator, made known through Jesus."[1]

---

1. Blaise Pascal, *Pensées* (New York: Penguin, 1997), 45.

Paul understood how crucial the feeding of his soul was to him that he was willing to lose everything that his contemporaries would consider prestigious for the supreme good of satisfying his soul. In Philippians 4, he stated:

> "Whatever gains I had, these I have come to consider a loss because of Christ. More than that, I even consider everything as a loss because of the supreme good of knowing Christ Jesus my Lord. For this sake I have accepted the loss of all things and I consider them also much rubbish, that I may gain Christ."

Feeding one's soul is not just an exercise of religious or non-religious, it is not an exercise of rich or poor; it is everyone's obligation. The soul is an essential part of the body that requires a specific form of treatment that is independent of the way we feel. You cannot take away the soul's lunch as a punishment for not getting the blessing you wanted.

It is important to understand that the cries of the body are not always audible. Some physical needs are very silent in nature while they are capable of bringing tears and sadness. We talked about that in a preceding chapter. This book does not advocate that Christians are unemotional beings that cannot become stressed, discouraged, or troubled. These emotions are a normal part of life. Christianity is not a trouble-free religion. In fact, Jesus who initiated this philosophy, did not call his followers to immune them from ever having any trouble. His death was not to make life easy for them. He said in John 16:33:

> "I have told you these things, so that in me you may have peace. In this world you will have trouble. But take heart! I have overcome the world.

What does that mean?

Jesus did not specify the type of trouble his disciples will face: emotional, physical, or mental. He only says that they will have trouble. What is important is that he offers a solution before the warning. *"In me...peace."* The solution to the problems that you will be facing is in *me*. This is exactly what Paul did: *he considered everything rubbish for the supreme good of knowing Christ.* Normally when problems come our way, we search horizontally for solutions; we move from one to the next until we find something that somewhat satisfies.

Antidepressant is irrelevant in the crying of the soul: it doesn't satisfy.

Suppose that someone had to cross a hot desert and a "friend" said to him: *since you have to cross that long desert and you don't have enough water, let me give you this pill to help quench your thirst.* He might think it is a great idea and rejoice that his problems are solved, since he won't have to worry about finding water anymore; but in fact, he has been given a death sentence. He might walk a few hours extra before he eventually collapses and dies. He didn't feel the thirst because he had shut his brain and organs down so they would not scream for help; they were forced to silently die of dehydration. This might sound cruel, but it is also true for pain and any other sensations. You can't conceal, or even replace the needs of the soul with something else and expect satisfaction. Antidepressants that are often used as a remedy are irrelevant in answering the crying of a soul; they do not satisfy. The pill temporarily quenched the thirst but did not prevent the body from dying of a greater problem. Likewise, antidepressants provide a short-term relief to a problem that becomes bigger when the effect of the drug is gone. Pills or therapy do not and cannot solve the problem of a thirsty soul. Jesus says that *you may have peace in me.* The cure for depression or trouble is peace. Since a hungry soul can be evidenced through loneliness or anxiety: the solution is to flood the soul with the presence of Christ.

In the second part of the verse, Jesus also told his followers to be courageous during their pilgrimage. The life of a believer can be compared to a bus ride; sometimes smooth, sometimes rough and rugged. The driver put a sign at the door for everyone to see: *"The ride is not going to be always smooth; there are going to be some rough times as well. Be courageous, for I am an experienced driver."* Almost every passenger had the opportunity to either read or have someone read it to him/her. Yet, at the first bump, they yell, and scream; some even accuse the driver of not being competent. The driver never promised only a smooth ride; he only said that he would be a source of peace when the ride gets rough. In other words, they need to keep their eyes on the driver who promised a safe ride. A safe ride does not mean trouble-free; it means a certainty to make it to the other side.

DISCUSSION QUESTIONS

1. What verse in the Bible would you say encourages us to feed the soul?

_____

_____

2. Since the cry of the soul is silent, how would you detect it?

_____

_____

3. Do you ever feel depressed and lonely? What do you do then?

_____

_____

4. How would you describe your ride? Is it bumpy or smooth?

_____

_____

5. How confident are you of the driver's competence?

_____

_____

UNDERSTANDING
THE LANGUAGE OF THE SOUL

God created man in three parts: the body, the soul, and the spirit; each unit contains its own means of communication. The body communicates with the material (world consciousness), the spirit with God (God consciousness), and the soul serves as a bridge between the body and the spirit; it has two lines of communication. The soul communicates with the spiritual world through the spirit, and the physical world through the body; it is the center of knowledge, the intellect. The soul is connected to the body and the spirit, it is the strongest of the three, it reflects man's personality. The spirit is connected to God, but it does not have the power to transfer that info to the body; it must use an interpreter: the soul. The body, which is the house of all emotions, doesn't speak the language of the spirit. It also relies on the soul, the domain of the self. In 2 Corinthians 2:14, we read:

> The person without the Spirit does not accept the things that come from the Spirit of God but considers them foolishness, and cannot understand them because they are discerned only through the Spirit.

The soul which is located between the two worlds has a normal tendency to agree with the needs and the desires of the body; it easily connects with the world. It must be trained and sometimes ordered to obey or speak the language of the spirit. David, in Psalm 103, had to order his soul to be grateful to God: "Bless the Lord, O my soul: and all that is within me bless his holy name."

The soul, being the center of man's personality, has the authority to decide whom he wants to yield to: the spirit or the body. It can be a materialist or a God-fearing arbiter. When it leans more toward the material, the Bible says that it is: *Governed by the flesh, it is hostile to God; it does not submit to God's law, nor can it do so.* (Romans 8:7). This means that it is in a state of constant hostility with God; it lets the soul starve for spiritual nourishment while allowing the body to enjoy a lavishly free ride. On the other hand, when the soul stands between the body and the spirit as a "God fearing arbiter", it yields this leadership authority to the spirit and the emotions take their cues from the spirit.

We have such an example in the book of Luke, Chapter 10. Jesus sent seventy-two of his disciples out to preach; they returned with joy and told the master that: *Even the demons submit to them in his name.* Jesus said that he saw Satan fall like lightning, that he has given them authority to trample the enemy but most importantly he said they should rather rejoice that their names are written in the book of life. Right after, the Bible says that:

> "Jesus, full of joy through the Holy Spirit said: 'I praise you, Father, Lord of heaven and the earth, because you have hidden these things from the wise and learned, and revealed them to little children...'" (Luke 10:21)

Please notice the source of this joy; it channeled its way to the body "*through*" the Holy Spirit. In other words, the Spirit bypassed the soul and directly communicated his joy to the body. Intimacy with God can be so passionate that the spirit doesn't have to wait for an authorization from the soul to transmit his expression of joy or sadness to the body. The Bible calls that: "*Being filled with the Holy Spirit*" (Luke 4:1); the Holy Spirit filled him so much that his soul could not contain it. Jeremiah had a similar experience and he reported it in Jeremiah 13.

> "If you do not listen, I will weep in secret because of your pride; my eyes weep bitterly, overflowing with tears, because the Lord's flock will be taken captive." (Jeremiah 13:17)

The tears of the prophet are in reflection and a response to the sadness of the Lord in the face of the stubborn and defiant attitude of his people who are about to experience deportation. Jeremiah is so connected with the Lord that God's disappointment becomes his.

Another example is in Luke chapter 1 when Mary, the mother of Jesus went to visit Elizabeth who was pregnant. After she greeted her, Elizabeth rejoiced and praised the Lord for such a favor. Mary said in verse 46, *My soul doth magnify the Lord and my spirit hath rejoiced in God my Savior..."* (Luke 1:46,47, KJV) Please consider the verbs; the first one is present tense (*magnify*), the second (*rejoiced*) is in past tense. The tense seems to suggest that the spirit initiated the exultation and transmitted it to the soul which in turn expresses it through the organs of the body. Thus, one of the functions of the soul is to express God's word. Its purpose is to connect the material with the spiritual; it feeds on the word of God. When it is left starving for nourishment, it screams with desperation. In Psalm 43, David felt that dejection; he said: *"Why, my soul, are you downcast? why so disturbed within me?"* (Psalm 43:5). The Liberty Bible Commentary describes it in these terms: *Why has my soul been brought so low.* This form of agony is common to a malnourished soul; we just don't know how to listen to it. David understood the language of the soul and suggested *hope in the Lord* as the ultimate solution. He said *to go to the sanctuary in Jerusalem, to meet the living God. That is the source of enormous joy.* He believes that meeting with the Lord can lift up his spirit; it can restore peace to his troubled heart. Anyone who remains silent in the presence of the Lord, attentive to hearing the reverberating and sometimes desperate voice of the soul will perceive these words: *Seek me while I may be found; call on me while I am near.* (Isaiah 55:6) He is knocking at the door of your heart; he is whispering into your soul how much he loves you. Would you respond? He promises peace to whomever does.

ATTITUDE
ON ROUGH ROAD

Do not let your heart be troubled.

Trust in God, and trust also in me

—JOHN 14:1

The heart is afraid of the unknown, it feels uncomfortable and insecure when it must adventure through it. In John 14, Jesus is trying to settle the emotions of the disciples and he uses one word: *"Trust."* This is similar to a driver who is trying to convince passengers to venture on a journey with him.

1. He might talk about his credential

2. The importance of the trip

The Lord is not asking anyone to trust him without any records to support his claims. Psalm 24 and John 1:1 state that God founded the earth and everything else. He is not someone who has the power to create but is powerless to control that creation. A chemist may combine two chemicals to produce a disease but is unable to find a cure. The Bible says that our God created this world several thousand years ago and is still in full control of it. Normally, before we hire someone for a job, we look at his credentials. If the records show that he is experienced, he gets the job; if not, we look for someone else. The Lord wants to be our shepherd but first, he gives us full access to his records.

If you are on a rough road and your heart is troubled with uncertainty, let's look at the driver's records.

Are you troubled with the weather?

Luke 8:22–25 tells us that Jesus has power over nature. He was on the lake with the disciples, and he fell asleep when a sudden squall came down on them. The disciples, afraid, woke him up. *He got up and rebuked the wind and the raging waters, they subsided, and all was calm.* If your fear is death, let me remind you that he rose a man to life four days after he was dead. (John 11:38–43); better yet, he rose from the dead three days after his own death. (Acts 10:40) What troubles you on the road? Is it Satan and his demons? Luke 8:26–33 tells us that Jesus handled a legion at once; when he was about to cast them away, they begged him to let them enter into a flock of swine. Are you stressed about your ability to provide for your family? My goodness, look at Luke 9:10–17. He fed several thousands of people all at once with five breads and two fishes; he is certainly capable of providing for your family and mine. He healed many from incurable diseases, walked on water, opened the eyes of blinds and many other miracles that couldn't be reported. Look at his credentials and after a thorough evaluation of his experiences, then you judge whether the bumps on your road are too big a challenge for him.

Is your cup overflowing with sorrow, are you struck with disease and your friends have abandoned you, is the enemy called you a failure, did you lose your job, do you feel that you are slowly sliding down the slope of depression, are you feeling suicidal? Please do not be fooled to think that a better job, drug or even a friend will give happiness. Many who went that route ended up being so disappointed that they killed themselves. If you have too many bumps on your road, feel scared, and don't know if you should trust him, look at his record. Every promise he made thus far has been fulfilled and the place where he vows to take us is worth every pain we may encounter on the way.

If you feel at the lowest pit and no one seems to care, it is time to begin praising the Lord. Don't wait till you get out, it might be too late; we were created for that purpose. As you begin praising him, you will find contentment; John 16:33 tells us that Jesus wants us to have peace even in the midst of a troubled world. Someone else might be right now at the top of his career, everything seems to rotate around him. He is honored, respected, loved, praised, and wealthy; he is surrounded by great minds, yet, he is slowly being taken away by death. None of his fame or wealth, or power or friends can stop it. But you, take a look at your past, how many times have you come close to death? How many times has the enemy said it is over? You are still alive, and well. That reminds me of what Jesus said to Simon:

> Simon, Simon, Satan has asked to sift all of you as wheat. But I have prayed for you, Simon, that your faith may not fail. (Luke 22:31, 32a)

I pray that the Lord keeps your faith strong, don't let your circumstances determine your mood or affect your relationship with the master. You are precious in the sight of God. In 1 Chronicles 16:21,22, God said that *He will allow no one to oppress his people; for their sake he rebuked kings*: He further said:

> "Do not touch my anointed ones."

Feeding one's soul is not based on your achievement, your success, your bank account, or your blessings; it is a duty. We were created for that purpose. When the soul doesn't get its food, it cries out and this reflects on our emotions. Refusal to feed the soul is the perfect recipe for depression. The same way pain is a benefit to the body, depression is a benefit to the soul. If you were playing soccer and broke a toe, without pain you will continue playing until your foot falls off. Likewise, without depression to warn of the necessity to feed the soul, the person may fall into (MDD) Major Depressive Disorder which is a mood disorder characterized by: Fatigue, feeling of worthlessness, difficulty concentrating, and even suicidal thoughts. Don't let the world offer you pills to quiet it down. It is a normal sensation that God created to inform his people about the state of the soul. No doctor can examine your soul and tell you the state of its health; the ultimate medication to keep the soul healthy is the word of God.

Even if you were in a position where you don't have the means to provide nourishment for the body, feed the soul; it is free. God will notice your obedience and will provide for the body; he is *Jehovah-Jireh*. Psalm 34 says:

> "The powerful grow poor and hungry, but those who seek the Lord lack no good thing." (Psalm 34:11)

When your soul is hungry, remember Jesus' advice: you can't satisfy the cry of the soul apart from the Bread of Life.

> "I'm the bread of life." Jesus said. "He who comes to me will never go hungry, and he who believes in me will never be thirsty. (John 6:35)

> May the God of hope fill you with all joy and peace as you trust in him, so that you may overflow with hope by the power of the Holy Spirit (Rom 15:13)

DISCUSSION QUESTIONS

1. Write down your own experience with depression

_____

_____

2. Is it difficult to trust the driver when the road gets rough?

_____

_____

3. Do you feel downcast and rejected? Read Psalm 43 and write your emotions after.

_____

_____

4. What is intimacy with God? How do we cultivate that?

_____

_____

5. What do you do when you feel depressed?

_____

_____

Bibliography

Alper, Joseph. "Depression at an Early Age." *Science* (May, 1986): 45–50.

Block, Susan. "Assessing and Managing Depression in the Terminally Ill Patients." *Ann Intern Med* 132 (3) (2000): 209–18.

Briggs, Megan. "Why are Pastors depressed? A look at the research." September 23, 2019. CHURCHLEADERS.COM. https://churchleaders.com/news /359562-why-are-pastors-depressed-a-look-at-the-research.html.

Chateaubriand, René, *Les Grands Ecrivains Français*. New York: Holt, Rinehart and Watson, 1965.

———. *Memoirs Beyond the Grave*. New York: NYREV, Inc., 2018.

Frank, et al. *Archives of General Psychiatry* 47 (1990): 1093ff.

Gary, J. K., Howard R. K., Cynthia.T., Wendy W., Helen M., and Polly E. B. "Hierarchy of Characteristics Associated with Depressive Symptoms in an Urban Elderly Sample." *American Journal of Psychiatry* 146(2): 220–25.

Kimmel, P.L., K. Weihs, and R.A. Peterson. "Survival in Hemodialysis Patients: The Role of Depression." *Journal of the American Society of Nephrology* 4 (1) (1993): 12–27.

Lewin, Bertram D. "Réflexions sur la depression." *Revue Française de psychanalyse* Vol.68 (2004/4): 1073–84.

Muñoz, R. F., and J. Miranda. *Group Therapy Manual for Cognitive-Behavioral Treatment of Depression*. Santa Monica: Rand, 2000.

Musset, Alfred de. *Tristesse*. Gauthier.

Neporent, Liz. "What Happens When a Plane's Cabin Depressurized Loss of cabin pressure triggers confusion before sleepiness and even death" September 5, 2014. abcnews.go.com. https://abcnews.go.com/Health/ planes-cabin-depressurizes/story?id=25277752.

Pahlajani, S., and S. Najjar. "Inflammation and Immunity in Depression." *Elsevier International Journal* (2018).

Pascal, Blaise. *Pensées*. New York: Penguin, 1997.

Rathje, Steve. "Don't Say That Depression Is Caused by Chemical Imbalance." *Psychology Today*, August 9, 2018. https://www.psychologytoday.com/ us/blog/words-matter/201808/dont-say-depression-is-caused-chemical- imbalance.

Rosenfield, Anne H. "Depression: Dispelling Despair." *Psychology Today* (June: 1985): 28.

Seligman, Martin E. P. *Learned Optimism.* New York: Alfred A. Knopf, 1991.

Sidebothan, Steven E., Martin Hense, and Hendrikje M. Nouwens. *The Red Land: The Illustrated Archeology of Egypt's Eastern Desert.* Cairo: The American University in Cairo Press, 2008.

Simon, Gregory E., Michael VonKorff; William Barlow. *Archives of General Psychiatry* 52 (10) (1995): 850–56.

Sproul, R. C. "Spiritual Depression: The Dark Night of the Soul." In *Tabletalk Magazine*, August 7, 2019. https://www.ligonier.org/blog/the-dark-night-of-the-soul/.

Szczygiet, B., B. Wanot, and M. Magerčiakova. "Depression Definition, History of Views, Recognition." *Scientific Journal of Polonia University* 30(5) (2018): 99–106.

Wells, K. B., et al. "The Functioning and Well-being of Depressed Patients." *Journal of the American Medical Association* 262(7): 914–919.